Table of Contents

Introduction

Parenting is the hardest full-time job you will ever take on. By full-time, I mean that parenting is twenty-four-seven, three-hundred-sixty-five. Even if you get a day off where your child is staying with grandparents or a friend or at summer camp, you will probably still have to perform parenting duties. Working this hard can sometimes make you feel like your brain is frying, and other times it can make you feel unappreciated and undervalued. After all, you're actually spending money on this job, rather than getting paid for it, and you don't have any paid time off! On top of that, you also probably worry that you are not doing a good job. There is certainly no easy, comprehensive guide letting you know if you are on the right track or not and answering your every question clearly. There is also always the chance that you are making some mistakes.

But being a parent does not have to drive you crazy. Take a deep breath. Step back. Understand that your mistakes are not life or death and that you are doing your best, which is more than good enough. Also realize that you are still a human being with needs that sometimes need to come first. It is OK to be selfish and to demand some things for yourself. You don't give up your identity with the birth of your child.

Do you feel better already? Good. I certainly hope so. You deal with enough craziness as a parent. You deserve to feel rested and relieved for once.

Now this good, rested, relieved feeling needs to become habit for you. You need to start putting yourself first sometimes, instead of dedicating literally all of your resources and time to your child or children. This book is your guide on how to take care of yourself and preserve your sanity as an undervalued, underpaid, extremely hard worker. This book will show you how to navigate parenting with a clearer head and a greater sense of peace.

This book does not have all the answers to your great parenting questions. It won't be able to tell you which decision to make when you reach a confusing crossroads in your parenting. But it will help you make decisions with a clearer mind and more grounded attitude. It will also help you feel better about yourself and your parenting techniques. Finally, it will show you how to love yourself and take time for yourself, which will ultimately make you a better parent to your child or children. So if you want to feel better and become a better parent, you have picked up the right book.

Happy reading!

Chapter 1: How Parenting Can Make You Feel Crazy

I can assure you that the way you feel right now is totally normal. Plenty of other parents feel the same way that you do, they just don't discuss it openly. Nobody tells you just what to expect as a parent, or they try to tell you but you can't fully picture what they are saying until you become a parent yourself. You have probably already encountered plenty of surprises, some great and some...not so great. The one thing that you now see is that people were not joking when they said that parenting is the sweetest gift and the hardest challenge that you will ever face in the course of your life.

One thing you probably did not count on was feeling like you are losing your mind. Well, this, too, is normal. You are not going to have an easy time of it, no matter how old your child is. The sense of losing your mind is quite normal and quite common.

Why do you feel this way? You may wonder that. Here are some common reasons that parenting is making you feel like you are crazy:

Over-exhaustion. You may feel exhausted. And, indeed, parenting is a tough and exhausting job. You may not be getting enough sleep as you stay up all night trying to comfort a crying newborn with colic, or helping your child fall asleep because he is scared of the monster under the bed. If you work or have to keep up a house or have other duties on top of taking care of your child, you have a full plate. It may be hard to get enough sleep. It may even be hard to fall asleep, as you have difficulty turning your mind off with all of the stress and worry that you endure every day.

The best thing to do is to get your child on a strict sleep schedule. This makes it easier for your child to fall asleep. It also gives you a regular schedule so that your mind knows when to finally turn off. There will still be sleepless nights but you will find that a regular bedtime will improve your sleep as well as your child's. Be sure to avoid eating or feeding your child at least five hours before bed. Also avoid caffeine after six. Try to limit the amount of sugar and caffeine that your child consumes, as well.

Keeping things regular and consistent throughout the day also helps when it comes to bedtime. Your child knows what to expect throughout the day, which helps him or her behave in a calmer manner. When it comes to bedtime, your child knows that it is time to go to sleep.

It is acceptable to be very strict about bedtime. Do not let your child stay up. You can offer consequences if your child keeps waking up or coming into your room throughout the night. It may seem cruel, but you are actually doing yourself, your partner, and your child a favor by not allowing the all-night dance.

Fighting. You know what's best for your kids because you have learned the hard way, through experience, and you have been taught by your own parents. But your child always has to disagree. You must fight with your child to get him to eat vegetables, to take vitamins, to drink adequate amounts of water, to go to bed, to not watch shows that will give him nightmares later, on and on and on. Sometimes it may feel like a losing battle. Sometimes you may feel like you are at your wit's end trying to get this kid to stay healthy and on a good track! No matter what age your child is, you probably have to fight him to do what's best and you probably find him doing the opposite of what you say quite a bit. This can get even worse as a child grows older.

While there is no single way to end the fight, the best thing to do is to never back down. The minute you back down, your child learns that he can have his way. If you hold your ground, you teach him to respect you and listen to you. In time, he will probably learn to listen better.

You also need to ease up a bit. Relax. The bad things in the world sometimes need to be experienced just as much as the good. Let your child live a little and experience life as it really is. It's a valuable growing up experience for him. You don't have to monitor everything he does or protect him from everything out there in the world.

Worry. Parenting is a very anxiety-inducing task. There are many dangers out there, and you must be vigilant at all times. Worry is the sign of a good parent who cares, but it can also wear down your nervous system and make you miserable. If you are a very anxious parent, you worry too much. You wish you could turn your mind off, but you can't, so you continue to suffer horribly. The worst part is that this worry never goes away with time. Your child will always matter to you, and hence you will always feel anxiety and you will always worry about him.

It is best to release some of this worry and anxiety. While it is a good thing to be careful and cautious, worrying too much accomplishes nothing besides hurting you. Too much anxiety and stress over time can lead to health problems. Your anxious parenting style is also teaching your child to worry in an unhealthy way. It is best to realize that all of this worry is unnecessary, and let it go. Try mindfulness meditations and yoga to calm yourself down. There are even forms of yoga designed for mothers to do with their children.

Not Enough Space. Part of becoming a parent calls for sacrifice of your space, personal time, and even hobbies. You may feel like you are losing part of your identity, however, as you give up everything to spend time with your child. You will encounter times when you can't even have five minutes in the bathroom alone. Your child is always talking to you or needing something from you, and while you don't mind providing for your child, sometimes you just want a few minutes alone or in silence so that you can hear yourself think! This extends to children never letting you talk on the phone or go out.

It is OK to set boundaries and demand some time for yourself. Having a kid does not mean that you need to lose your identity or who you are. You are entitled to some free time and space away from your child. Make this space mandatory and set aside some time for you every day, where your child is napping, with a sitter or family, or with your spouse. Even if you just ask for five minutes to take a quick shower in peace, you deserve this time to yourself. Your life should not be ruled by this little human being. While he is precious and you do love him, you also need to take care of yourself. By doing so, you are actually teaching your child healthy coping skills for when he becomes a parent and you are teaching him that his own health and sanity should remain a priority for him.

Make it a hard and fast rule that your child cannot bother you while you are speaking on the phone. He may not interrupt; instead, he should touch you lightly to indicate that he has something to say, and then he needs to wait. Also make it a rule that nobody can disturb you while you in the bathroom, unless it is a matter of life or death. Teach your child to entertain himself with games and toys so that he is not constantly dependent on you for entertainment.

Tension with Your Partner. Whether you are with your child's other parent or not, having a child can create a lot of tension and friction in your relationship together. You may have disagreements about custody if you are split up, or you may have disagreements about how to raise your child. You may quarrel about splitting chores or spending time with your child together. In addition, exhaustion and hormones from having a baby can negatively impact your sex life and make intimate time difficult. While raising a child together, it may be hard for you two to find time for dates and special time together.

This is perfectly normal. But this tension can add to the stress that you are already experiencing and make you feel awful. You must take care of your partner and your relationship as much as possible. Make your partner a priority and never sacrifice his or her needs for that of your child. Treat him or her as important. Make time for love and romance, even if you are utterly exhausted. And more than anything, approach this as a team effort that you are both in on.

If you and your child's parent are separated, it may be even harder to stay on the same page and keep your feelings in check. Fighting, miscommunication, and other problems may abound. However, if you keep in mind that your child's rearing is the most important job that you two must complete together, then you can more effectively set your feelings aside and work well with your partner. Always approach your relationship from the point of view that you are both here to do what you can for your child. Try not to focus on your own feelings, as hard as that may be.

Weird...Stuff. There is no other way to describe it. Sometimes your child does weird stuff that you are not prepared to deal with. Each child in the world is unique, and they come up with odd and crazy things as they grow and explore the world around them. Sometimes, they come up with very odd problems that no other child seems to have. They may ask you weird questions like, "What would happen if my head exploded?" They may ask you about sex or they may engage in masturbation. They may invent disturbing and even violent games with their friends and their toys. Once or even more than once, they may get into trouble at school for fighting, bullying, inappropriate behavior, lewd references, or even crimes like shoplifting. You may wonder with panic if your child is all right, and chances are, he is just fine. Children are constantly growing and experimenting, so even their odd or disturbing phases are usually just part of their long and gradual journey into adulthood. Along this journey, they may do inexplicably weird things, they may behave badly, and they may even commit crimes.

Nevertheless, you will probably be surprised often and sometimes even disturbed at times as a parent. You may worry that you are doing a bad job and that something is wrong with your child or your parenting skills. These moments can make you feel powerless and insecure. Don't let them bother you too much, however. Take these weird moments as a sign that your child is finding himself and learning about the world. It is all going to be OK.

Of course, you should never ignore your gut. If you feel that something is truly wrong, listen to that concern. After all, you know your child best and you can tell when something is wrong. So many parents ignore their gut and hence they do not find out if their children have autism, learning disabilities, speech impediments, or psychiatric issues so that they cannot address these issues early on. Take your child to some sort of counselor or talk to him yourself. Get him tested for learning disabilities or growth issues, if you feel that his development is not normal. Address any issues that you find particularly disconcerting or distressing right away.

Jealousy and Resentment. Yes! This does happen! You may feel petty and childish for feeling jealous as you perceive that your partner treats your child more sweetly than he or she treats you, but this feeling does happen rather often!

It is important to remember that you are not the only one in the picture anymore. While jealousy and resentment of your child are common, you should not give into these feelings or let them dictate your actions as a parent.

Repetition. We all know how repetitive kids can be. As they learn, they tend to repeat things. You may hear the same songs or the same phrases repeated constantly over a rather lengthy period of time. This kind of repetition is enough to drive anyone crazy. You are not a bad parent for feeling this way. However, you must remember that repetition is normal and a part of your child's development and learning.

It is best to have a sense of humor about all things kid-related. You are not in total control. You are not perfect, and neither is your kid. Your child is sometimes annoying and weird, as much as you love him unconditionally. Just laugh things off and save them in your memory bank. You never know what will make a hilarious story to tell at your child's wedding later on!

Post-partum Depression. Post-partum depression is a sad reality that afflicts many mothers. You enter motherhood expecting to be overjoyed and happy, and instead you feel miserable. You may not feel any love for your child; this is not because you are an evil person, but because your hormones are out of balance and you are not feeling right. Seek immediate treatment. Once you cure your depression, you will find that motherhood is much easier and you do have plenty of love for your child.

Personality Conflicts. Your child may be fifty percent you, but there is a good chance that he is nothing like you. You may love him, but you may also find it difficult to get along with him. It is perfectly normal for your child to have a vastly different personality and nature from you, and for that difference to lead to conflict.

The best thing to do is to learn as much as you can about your child's personality type. Look into the Meyers-Briggs personality index and figure out what personality type your child falls into. Then, you can learn from the personality description how your child will act. Anticipating how your child will react to certain things can help you understand how to prevent conflict and how to keep from fighting or disagreeing with your child too much.

Also understand that you are here to be a parent, not a best friend. You don't have to like your child like a friend would, you just have to love him and provide him with solid guidance. Chances are, he will grow into a great person that you will get along with great. It is normal to not get along well with a child, particularly an adolescent, but never let that interfere with your love.

Favoritism. Sadly, we all want to be perfect parents. But none of us are perfect. Scientists have discovered that parents do indeed have favorites. If you find yourself favoring one child over another, this is perfectly normal. However, this favoritism can really hurt your least favorite child's self-esteem. You really do need to show your love to both of your children.

Try to hide this favoritism and treat your children equally. Spend equal amounts of time with both or all of your children, and don't ever play favorites. Make sure that the punishments you dole out are equal and fair, not based on which child you tend to side with. If you notice that you are starting to show favoritism to one child over another, make up for it by taking your other child out for ice cream.

It is also common for a parent to bond more with same-sex children than opposite-sex children. So if you happen to favor a son or daughter more because you share a gender, remember that this is normal and does not make a bad person. But you need to spend equal amounts of time with both children. Try to find activities that you can all enjoy together, regardless of gender.

Disappointment. This is another feeling that is sadly common among parents, though no one likes to admit to it. You may have big plans or dreams for your kid, and you feel let down or disappointed when your child does not live up to your expectations.

While it may sounds terrible to say this, you should keep your expectations of your child low. Focus more on helping him excel as a good person with integrity and focus on helping him do well in school. Don't expect him to magically excel at sports just because you did or you always wanted to. Don't put dreams on him that are your dreams, not his. Notice when he excels at something that is difficult for him, such as spelling or making a shot in basketball, and praise him for his feats instead of scolding him for not doing what you wanted. This way, you will not be disappointed. Your child also will not feel like a failure to you and will not develop severe self-esteem issues.

Too Much Responsibility. Sometimes, you may feel that you are overloaded with responsibility. You may have work, parenting duties, household chores, cooking, etc. There is just not enough time in the day to get everything on your to-do list done before bedtime, it may seem. A lot of parents feel this way because parenting is a huge responsibility, on top of the other things that you must contend with in your life. But there is no need to overload yourself.

Take a look at your schedule. Is there anything that you can cut back on or cut out altogether? A lot of things that you stress about and try to get done are actually not important in the grand scheme of things and can be forgotten or postponed. Also work on managing your time better and living by a fairly strict routine. Keep track of appointments in a planner and set alarms and reminders on your phone. Accept that you are not perfect and let some things go. You don't have to be Supermom or Superdad. In addition, while it may seem counter-intuitive, you will find that taking some time off to just relax and spend time with your family helps you manage your time better. Relaxation helps you handle yourself and your time better, while time that you spend with your family is time that is never wasted.

Childhood Wounds. A bad childhood will leave wounds on your psyche. You will often have to confront these wounds as a parent. You will have to fight the urge to act like your own parents did, and you will have to continually relive memories of your childhood as you watch your own child grow up. Being a parent has the surprising consequence of making you face your own demons head-on.

Counseling or therapy is never a bad idea if you have many childhood wounds to heal. If you suffered abuse as a child, you have learned a lot of bad parenting habits and you have sustained tremendous injury to your self-esteem and self-image. Therapy can help you work through that. Also try to keep a journal to work out your thoughts and remind yourself that you are better than your parents were. If you feel that you are unable to be an adequate parent, you can take a parenting class to learn great skills and anger management.

Therapy is not for everyone. You can do your own therapy by practicing cognitive-behavioral therapy, also known as CBT. CBT is where you identify your own bad thought patterns and correct them into healthier patterns. You should perform research into this method and start employing it today to feel better about yourself and become a better parent.

Aggression and Misbehavior. Not all kids are perfect. Ideally, though, your children are well-behaved, respectful, and quiet. If your child is not those things, then you may feel that you are losing your mind as you fight with your child and try to remedy his behavior. Your child may be a great person at heart, but he acts out inappropriately and can't seem to learn respect for his elders. He may mean well, but it comes out wrong. He may be spastic, hyper, aggressive, or a number of other things that are not good.

The best thing to do is to not fight your child's natural personality. Instead, teach your child how to hone his natural traits into strengths that will serve him well in life. For instance, if your child is aggressive, show him how he can use that for being ruthless in business as opposed to being mean in his personal relationships. Praise him for his good qualities and focus on those, as well, so that he learns to grow and develop those traits instead of the bad ones. Offer more rewards for good behavior than punishments for bad behavior. Of course, you should also learn some good discipline techniques to help your child learn which behaviors are unacceptable with poor consequences and which behaviors are possible to condone.

True problem children are out there. If your child is one, then understand that there is still hope. You may blame yourself, but it is not always your fault. A large number of factors may cause your child's outbursts and misbehavior. Consider attending child therapy together or get your child active in a sport to teach him discipline, respect, and patience. Martial arts is a great way to keep kids active while teaching them to focus and be mindful of how their actions affect others. Often, spending some time with your child just playing ball or going shopping together can have tremendous power over transforming his behavior. Also try talking with him and finding out what is bothering him and causing him to act out. An open relationship of sharing and trust is essential for you to establish with your child. Instead of making him fear the consequences of punishment, let him feel that he can talk to you and turn to you for help when life gets tough.

Other Life Events. Life doesn't magically stop once you have a child. No, it goes on, and you will have other things to deal with on top of the duties of parenting. You may encounter tragedies, losses, or other conflicts in life that bring you considerable emotional strife. You have to deal with this pain on top of raising your child. You may feel that you are losing your mind as you try to keep it together and remain strong for your family, while your heart is breaking inside your chest.

The most important thing to keep in mind in these situations is that you are only human. You are just as allowed to have emotions as the rest of your family. Demonstrating these emotions will not scar or hurt your child. In fact, coping with your emotions in a healthy way and addressing them head-on instead of repressing and hiding them will set a healthy model for your child to learn from. Don't repress your emotions for the sake of your family. Let your emotions out and heal with your family's help.

In addition, your family may be suffering and grieving as well. Don't ignore your feelings to take care of theirs. Instead, hold each other and support each other in your pain. Use each other to heal. Getting through tragedies together and speaking openly together about your feelings and grief processes will make you all stronger and closer. It will also make healing much easier. Best of all, you will be teaching your children that they can talk to you when they are upset or grieving in the future. Grieving together will feel better than crying alone in your bedroom or the bathroom after your kids are asleep.

Bad Support. Some people are just jerks. Some people don't have any clue about how hard the job of parenting really is. As a result, these people fail to offer you any support. They simply don't seem to understand what you are going through and they are unwilling to offer you reasonable accommodations. These people may include stringent bosses who don't see why you need time off when your baby is sick, in-laws or family members who don't understand why you can't fly halfway across the country with a hyper toddler, or friends who don't get why you have to cancel plans because you are unable to find a sitter.

It is best to not let these people get to you. Try to find a more accommodating job, if you can. Stop hanging out with pushy friends. Explain gently but firmly to family and co-workers why your child limits what you are able to do. You can be as firm as you want to, but losing your temper probably won't help. Most importantly, try to find other people who have or have had children to surround yourself with, as they will likely to be more understanding. Even if your boss continues to be difficult and unsympathetic, for example, you at least will have fellow parents in your friends group who will be able to commiserate with you. Also, you will probably find more people who are willing to help you out with babysitting and other things if you hang out with other parents.

Single Parenting. My hat goes off to all single parents out there. Single parents do indeed have it rough. If you are a single parent, you probably are experiencing nearly all of the stressors that I have just listed. On top of that, you are alone, working, and trying to raise a child or children without much or any assistance. Your struggles are profound and thus it is normal for you to feel like you are going crazy.

But you are not crazy. You are taking on a tremendous burden on your own. Try to spread the burden out by taking on the help of others. Build a good support network of other single parents, family, friends, reliable sitters, and other such people who can help you. These people can lighten the load that sits on your shoulders and help you feel more at peace. They can allow you to take a day off now and then, which everyone needs and deserves.

Also, remember that you are not Supermom or Superdad. You don't have to be. Just try your best. I guarantee that your best is more than enough for your child. Sitting down and reading a book to your child will more than make up for how much you have to work or other areas in parenting where you may feel that you are failing. You are probably not failing as much as you think. As long as you try to show your child how deeply you love him, you are still doing well as a parent.

Chapter 2: Step Back and Take a Breath

One of the hardest things to do when you are a parent is to just step back and take a deep breath. This advice may sound ridiculously simple, and that is because it is. Taking some time to relax and let go is easy. Finding the time and the wherewithal to do so is what is tough.

You are taking on a huge job and a huge burden. This burden is wonderful and you love your child, but you cannot deny that sometimes parental duties can feel more like a burden than anything. You deal with stress, worry, and fear all of the time for a variety of reasons, and rightly so.

But for once, what if you just let all that go? What if you closed your eyes, took a few deep breaths, and focused on feeling one with the moment? What if you gave yourself a break from all of this bad emotion?

Maybe the only time that you have to clear your mind is at bedtime. That is fine. Maybe get involved in meditating with your partner, or use earphones and listen to a meditation podcast or Youtube video. Do yoga or Tai Chi. Take a yoga class to get out of the house. Exercise is also helpful, and many gyms have day care centers. Just try to do something to take your mind off of worry and relax. Also, take care of your body. Parenting can age you so stress relief and exercise are very helpful in preserving your health and staying around to see your grandkids.

When you start to obsessively worry or feel anxious, remind yourself that this worry is not helping anyone. In fact, it is making you a more inaccessible and emotionally frigid parent. You want to be vigilant and take care of your child the best that you can, but don't spend too much time worrying excessively. Your child is tougher than you realize. He will be OK. The world is a scary place, but if you take precautions and remain vigilant, your child should be fine. Worry will not help protect him at all. It will only tax your mind and your body and make you more stressed, which impairs your ability to be a warm, emotionally available parent for your child.

Sometimes, all you need to do is repeat the mantra, "Everything will be OK." Tell yourself that when you begin to feel like an awful parent, or when you begin to worry a little too much about your child when he is out with friends or at school.

Chapter 3: Dealing with Frustration and Anger

Children are wonderful. They are precious gifts. But they can really make you mad. You can get extremely frustrated and angry as a parent. How can you handle this without taking it out on your child?

Here is a personal anecdote. A friend of mine was in a bad mood because she had been dealing with her seven-year-old son's constant nagging and hyperness all day long. She was exhausted and she started snapping at her child, without meaning to. Later, while putting away laundry in his room, she noticed that he had drawn a picture. She and her husband were represented as huge stick figures saying things like "Stop talking!", and then an arrow pointed to a miniscule stick figure standing between them with the caption "And me, the worst kid in the world." She realized how her snapping and anger was making her child feel like a bad kid. So she crossed out the mean words that she and her husband were depicted as saying and wrote instead, "You are the best kid in the world!" When he saw the picture, it made him very happy and he ran up and hugged his mom.

This story offers a powerful glimpse into how sensitive kids are, even if they don't show it. Your anger can have extremely detrimental effects. Watching your anger and releasing it in healthy ways is essential to being a good parent. Don't feel like a bad parent just because you get crabby and snappy. Just work on improving how you manage your anger.

Enlist Your Partner

You and your partner are in this together. Relying on one another to keep each other's anger in check is very helpful. Discuss how you can remind each other to take a step back and breathe. Use a sign or signal to indicate to each other to calm down.

Also, set clear guidelines for how you plan to discipline your child. Often parents are on different pages when it comes to discipline. You need to be on the same page. Decide what forms of discipline are OK and what forms are not. For instance, are you both OK with spanking? Are you comfortable with grounding? Have a discussion to decide discipline when your child does something bad, too. Don't just discipline your child as you see fit without first consulting your partner. Expect your partner to always consult you first, too.

Take a Breath Before You Speak

When you feel like you are about to get angry, take a deep breath. Breathing does wonders to simmer your stress response down. Exhalations can help you release anger.

Have a Heathy Outlet

If anger is a problem for you, having a healthy outlet can be very beneficial. Have a way to release your anger. Some people find punching bags are helpful. Others like to do yoga to calm their nerves. Yet others like to talk it over with friends or family. Find what works for you. Use this outlet instead of taking your anger out on your child.

Set Limits to Your Anger

Set clear limits for yourself. Yes, you will get angry at times. And sometimes your child needs to see that his behavior is aggravating or hurtful, so that he can learn to adjust his behavior and become a conscientious adult. But you need to determine how far your anger can go and how much anger you can express. Draw the line at excessive yelling. Never curse at your child or call your child names. Don't make anger emotional abuse by trying to make your child feel guilty. Also don't let your anger last too long. Too much yelling or the silent treatment for days can be very emotionally harmful. It is up to you if you wish to employ spanking, but physical violence is never OK. Also, threats are rarely effective.

Remember Anger can Escalate

Expressing how upset you are can be a cathartic release. But it can also escalate a situation. Step back and think, "How will my anger solve this problem?" It is often better to approach discipline from a calm perspective. So it is often best to keep your anger to yourself, give yourself five minutes to cool down, and then react to your child's behavior calmly.

Sometimes, you just need to get away. Take some time off. Do a craft or go to a yoga class. Have your child spend some time at Gramma's. Doing this gives you time to cool down and figure out if you really need to be angry at your child. Some things can safely be let go.

Chapter 4: Making Time for Yourself

Many parents make the mistake of putting themselves last. While this self-sacrificing and selfless attitude is admirable and noble, you are not any use to your child if you are not doing well yourself. Taking care of yourself is essential when you are a parent. Don't ever forget to put yourself first sometimes and make time for yourself.

When you first bring a baby home from the hospital, things are often crazy. You will not have time for yourself as you and your partner try to get your baby on a regular sleep schedule. But do things get easier? Yes and no. Your child will continue to need time and will continue to consume a lot of your energy. Even when he or she starts school, you will still have to be involved with school activities, sports, homework help, picking up and dropping off, and even taking the day off to take care of your child when he is sick. Even when your child hits adolescence, you will still have to be very involved, perhaps more so in many ways. You can't keep putting off your own self-care until your child is older. You need to start today.

It can be very overwhelming at first to think about adding anything to your already-crammed schedule. As you watch supermoms who manage to work out at least an hour a day while raising three kids, you may feel very inadequate. The truth is, most parents are not able to accomplish everything in a day. Things are probably not all perfect in the houses of these fit supermoms, so don't be jealous. You don't have to be perfect and have a perfect body while raising children. That is not what I mean by making time for yourself. While going to the gym or working out at home is a fantastic idea that will preserve your health, you don't have to become perfect. Focusing on yourself a little bit is not calling for a huge self-improvement project.

What I mean by taking time for yourself is taking time to actually enjoy yourself. Take some time where you release stress, let go of your concerns and worries, and just enjoy yourself. Even if this time is simply spent soaking in a hot bath with wine, reading a few pages of a book without being interrupted, or going to a night out with your buddies, that is fine. Take some time for yourself to do what makes you happy. While having a child is probably the most joyous thing to ever happen to you, let's face it, the act of parenting is probably not going to make you happy all of the time. Just like work cannot make you happy all of the time. A hobby or time with friends is what can give you that fulfillment that you need.

Also, don't feel that you have to put your life on hold. It is OK to make some time for yourself to work on goals that are close to your heart. Work and career may need to be adapted to make time for your family, but you can still build a career and perform stellar work and accomplish career goals. Art projects may take twice as long, but you can still finish that masterpiece.

It is OK to be selfish sometimes. By being selfish and taking some time for yourself, you will return to your child rejuvenated and refreshed. You will be less prone to snapping and irritability. You will be more patient and serene. Getting away and being selfish is actually quite beneficial to those around you. People fail to realize this fact. If someone ever criticizes you for taking time off from parenting, don't listen or let them make you feel bad. You are actually doing your family a service.

Also, don't think that your child needs you 24/7. He is perfectly fine being watched by family or your partner for a while as you go tackle some projects or take a hot bath alone. He actually needs to learn that he cannot depend on any one person totally. This prepares him for that first day of day care or school when you will not be there for hours. Children who are used to being without their moms or dads for at least a few hours a day will adjust to day care and school with far less drama and emotional turmoil. They are also usually better adjusted socially and more at ease being independent. Seeing their parents have lives outside of family duties can also teach them to go after their own dreams, manage their time, and realize their potential to have families and careers simultaneously as well.

Stop neglecting yourself. Put yourself first sometimes. You will thank yourself for it. And your family will ultimately thank you too, even if they whine and grumble and cry at first.

Chapter 5: Finding Time with Your Partner

It is so important to never neglect your romantic partner. Sadly, when you are overwhelmed with parenting duties, you may not have as much time or as much energy for love. Many couples make the mistake of forgetting about each other and neglecting their relationship while they work on raising their children. Remember that your relationship with your partner is the most important thing in your life. Without this relationship, your child would not exist. Therefore, your relationship is of paramount importance and deserves attention and maintenance.

In addition, your relationship with your significant other sets the model for how your child will approach relationships. You don't want to set a poor model by ignoring or neglecting your significant other. Instead, you want to teach your child to cherish his or her future partner by cherishing your own.

Taking care of your relationship also helps you preserve your own sanity. If you ever feel like you are alone or you are losing your mind, you need to remember that you actually are not alone. Your partner is right there, in the same boat as you. You can lean on your partner for help. But in order to have this kind of relationship, you must keep your partner around. You must continue to show him or her love and devotion. You must set some time aside for your relationship. Keep the romance alive.

How to Find Time for Romance

It isn't always feasible to just go out on a date. Finances might be tight or you two might be exhausted with a new child. But it is important to remember that your relationship is just as important as your child. In fact, your child wouldn't be here otherwise. So you two need to take care of each other and make time for each other.

Sometimes, the only time you may have is right before bed. Even if you don't feel like sex, kissing and cuddling for a few moments will reinforce your love bond while helping you both relax. It can be nice to lay in each other's arms.

Some parents don't ever want to demonstrate affection in front of their children. If you don't feel comfortable with it, that is entirely up to you. However, demonstrating affection in front of your children can teach them what wholesome love looks like. Therefore, you can take advantage of time that you spend with your kids to show each other love. Hug, kiss, cuddle. You can cuddle while watching a movie with the whole family or you can hold hands and talk about your day as you take your kids for a walk in the park. Find all the time that you can throughout the day.

Set up a rule where your child may not enter your bedroom if you want to improve your sex life. You don't want sex to be interrupted by your child peeking in. You can also find other places to get it on, such as the shower. Being clever and creative is how you can keep your love life alive, even if you have a nosy child who threatens to walk in on you at any time. Sometimes, if possible, rent a room and hire a babysitter or leave your child with grandparents so that you can have an uninterrupted night for romance.

It doesn't take much time to at least show your partner that you love him or her. Cards, kisses, and asking your partner how his or her day went are activities that take a few seconds, but they mean the world to your relationship. Failing to do these things is what causes you and your partner to grow distant and even dissatisfied. Many people just don't make time for each other. They let work and children get in the way of their relationships. Don't make this mistake and contribute to the high divorce rates of the modern day.

How to Keep Romance Alive

Now keeping the romance alive is easier said than done. You don't always feel very sexy after you have just been cleaning up a toddler's milkshake throw-up. You don't always feel like a romantic candlelit dinner when you have been running on little sleep and working hard to take care of a screaming newborn with colic. Just having a kid or kids in the house may also zap the mood, as you know that you are likely to be interrupted having sex or trying to have a romantic date.

But you don't always have to go above and beyond to create romance with your partner. Sometimes, you just have to give him or her a kiss and say, "I love you, I appreciate all that you do, and I'm so glad you and our child is in my life. I couldn't do this without you." Consider telling your partner this in person or giving him or her a card.

When you can, bring your partner a little gift from your grocery shopping trip. Just taking care to stock his or her favorite snacks or soda is a romantic gesture in itself. Bring him or her a treat every now and then. Make his or her favorite meal for dinner. Present him or her with flowers at least once a month. These little gestures show that you are thinking of your partner, and that means a lot.

Another lovely gesture is to send your partner thoughtful and sweet texts throughout the day. Or you can spice things up by sending him or her racy texts while he or she is in the next room, at work, or out running errands. These texts will make your partner smile and will spice up your love life, without taking much time or revealing your sexier flirting to your kids.

Sneaking away for date night is also great. You both need a break and you need to spend time together. Hire a babysitter, rent a room, and just have the night to yourselves. You two might just want to spend the whole time sleeping!

You don't have to have lots of wild sex to still have a great bond. Just cuddling for a few minutes as you fall asleep, kissing each other good-bye and hello, and trying to be kind to each other and remember to have patience as you work at parenting together can be plenty of physical love to keep you two going. But when you do feel up to it, sex is important to most couples. You should always try to work up the energy to make love when you can. You may get into a loop where you claim that you are too tired, and you probably are tired, but if you at least try, you will find that sex actually gives you energy. Sex increases your bond but also helps you relax and feel good. It can make the stressful parts of parenting better as you make love and hold each other.

You should have an activity that you do with your partner, and another one that you do with the entire family. Triathlons, yoga, volunteering, and other pursuits are excellent for whole families to do together. You can take up a hobby or competitive sport with your partner. Just find something that you can do alone with your partner, and also with your partner and child or children. You want to keep your family as a whole unit, but you also want to honor your bond with your partner.

Co-Parenting

If you have split up with the child's parent and you two are trying to co-parent, I take my hat off to you. Co-parenting is difficult and tricky. It is hard to communicate well with someone who does not live in your house. It is also hard to overcome personal feelings of hurt, betrayal, jealousy, bitterness, and whatever else you two may feel about your split. If other parties are involved, such as a new partner or spouse, that can make wires cross even more.

Ideally, your child's other parent will be as interested in raising the child well as you are. He or she will continue to view you both as a team. You can talk to your child's other parent about this. It is best for you to put your differences aside and try your best to co-parent. When you have this talk, lay out some rules and determine how to stay in contact. Make it clear that communication is key.

It is OK to be leery of the other parent's new dating choices. You have every right to demand that you get to meet and speak to his or her new dates before you allow your child to go over there. An alarming amount of child abuse and sexual abuse is committed by people that the child knows. You want to limit the number of people who have access to your child, especially new people that your child is likely to trust. It is also OK for your child's other parent to demand the same thing of you. Don't take this as an insult to your choices in people or your judgment – take it as a sign that co-parenting is working and you both are invested in your child's health and safety.

When your child's other parent begins to get serious with someone new, it helps your child if you act like the bigger person and take the initiative. Introduce yourself and exchange phone numbers. Let the new girlfriend or boyfriend know that you simply want what's best for your child and you aren't trying to be threatening or over-involved. Suggest that all three of you spend time together bonding.

You also want to open the lines of communication with your child. Keep your child informed about the split and about your new arrangements with his other parent. This helps avoid anxiety. Setting up a good, reliable schedule with your co-parent is also essential to assuage your child's anxiety. You want to reassure your child that he is still very much loved and wanted by both of you, that the split is not because of him, and that you are both going to still be in his life. Let him know that he should talk to you, especially if someone in his other parent's home starts to mistreat him in any way. It is often recommended to teach your child the appropriate names for his anatomical parts and explain to him that no one but you and a doctor can touch those parts purely for health reasons, so that he can let you know if someone touched him inappropriately.

The best thing that you can possibly do for your child is to remain as a unit with your ex. Still go out as a family for dinner and the movies. Have a family game night that may or may not include stepchildren and step-parents. Do things together to keep up the idea that you are all still a family for your child. Even if you have lots of ill feelings for you ex, try to move past them.

When is it OK to limit contact between your child and his other parent? You can if drugs and alcohol are involved and his safety is threatened. You can if there has been a history of abuse. You can if you learn that your child is being mistreated. If your ex is not willing to become involved, you can let him or her make that choice, but be open to letting him or her see your child if he or she finally ever becomes willing to get involved. However, you should never use your child as a weapon to hurt your ex with. Your child's feelings are at play here. Your child is probably hurting too, and cutting off his contact with his other parent for no good reason can severely injure his self-esteem and his future relationships.

If Your Partner is not the Parent

Despite their bad reputation, step-parents are actually very admirable people. They step in and take over raising a child who is not theirs because they love you. They probably also come to love your child as their own. They may not be perfect, but they try.

If your partner is not the actual parent of your child, then you need to make some special considerations. It is crucial for you to show your partner that he or she is loved, wanted, and needed, even as a step-parent. Gestures of gratitude and appreciation will help him or her feel validated for his or her usually thankless work.

You also need to make sure to spend time with your partner. It is easy to leave a step-parent out as you struggle to spend time with your child and his other biological parent. Fitting everyone in your extended family into your schedule can be a special challenge. But as you attend events with your child's other family, spend time with your child, and talk to the other parent, you want to be careful not to make your new partner feel neglected. You want to show him or her that you still care. Lots of caring gestures and romantic gestures are essential to keep this relationship alive.

Encourage your child to act in a similar way. Tell him to thank your new partner for all that he or she does. Have him give your new partner gifts and make him or her cards. Feeling appreciation from your child will mean a lot to your partner and will show your partner that he or she is doing a good job that is not going unnoticed. Doing this also helps your child bond with your partner and get over any resentment that he may feel as a natural response to your separation from his biological parent.

Doing lots of family activities together is very important to help your child and partner bond. You can all go fishing, attend events together, or take a camping trip. Get involved in the same charities, sports, or other hobbies. You can really encourage your child to start to like your new partner.

It can be tricky to hash out parental duties. Just how much can your new partner discipline your child? Just how much parental authority does he or she have? You want to be fair to both your child and your partner. It is best to be very involved with your partner and set up clear guidelines for what he or she can and cannot do as a step-parent. Clear communication avoids a lot of the problems that mixed families face when it comes to discipline and child raising. Also, make it very clear how involved the other parent will be and try to work with both your ex and your partner to raise your child effectively. It is time to set personal feelings aside for the child's sake.

Don't feel bad for your partner's kindness and huge efforts to be part of the family. Your partner signed up for this because he or she wanted to. He or she is probably more than happy to assume parenting duties and work on building a family with you and your child. You are not taking advantage. However, you should strive to show your affection and gratitude at every turn. By doing this, you set the model for a good relationship to your child and you keep your partner around.

Chapter 6: Building a Better Bond with Your Child

One thing that can drive you crazy is if you don't have a truly strong and easy bond with your child. You may work too much or you may be separated from your child a lot because of a divorce or separation. You and your child may just not have an easy time bonding because of perfectly natural personality differences or ego clashes. For whatever reason, you and your child do not have the strong bond where you love spending time together, you know each other well, and you have open communication. This can hurt. You can feel inadequate as a parent, and you can worry that you are hurting your child and negatively impacting his development.

But that's all OK. It is never too late to strengthen your bond with your child. And it is possible to surmount the difficulties that have impeded your bonding experience in the past. Any effort that you make will show and your child will feel more loved as a result.

How can you start, though? You have probably tried everything and you feel that you are running into a brick wall time and again. Again, it is not too late, and you can find a way. Here are some suggestions to get you started on the right track.

Make Love into Action

Of course your child needs punishment for certain things. That doesn't mean that you don't love your child. But do you express your love for him often? You may think that it is implied, but it is not. When you discipline your kids a lot but don't take the time to say I love you and give them hugs, you send the harsh message that he is a bad kid who is not worthy of love. He may develop low self-esteem and attachment issues.

It is far better to follow up discipline with love. You will notice that you need to discipline a lot less when you start showing your kid love with hugs, kisses, and other gestures. Be sure to say "I love you" a lot.

Be More Mindful

You may think that you pay plenty of attention to your child. Is it mindful, quality attention though? Or are you busy looking at your phone, glancing at the TV, or thinking about work and barely paying attention to your child at all? In addition, how often do you dismiss your child while he tries to talk to you? You may mean to be nice, but you're overloaded and you unintentionally shut him out by saying things like, "Go sit over there and be quiet." "I can't deal with this right now. Can you talk about it later?" (and then you don't). And other things like this that pushes your child away and tells him that what he has to say is important.

You don't have to pay attention to your child all of the time. But be sure to dedicate some time to him, where it is just you two talking. Family dinner night, or better yet family game night and family activities, are even better. And please put your phone away for a while. Your Facebook and Twitter feeds will be there waiting for you later on, but your child grows up in the blink of an eye. In addition, life is more important than the digital world, so appreciate it by being fully present and mindful at least sometimes.

Never Break a Confidence

If your child comes to you and confides in you, you are bound by the power of the pinky swear. Unless you really have to take action, don't betray your child's trust. Keep his or her confidences safe, even from your partner. Your child will learn to trust you and to come to you in times of need.

Of course, there will be times when silence and secrecy is not OK. You need to speak out if your child alerts you to some sort of crime, abuse, drug use, or other issues. But in general, how important is something? How important will it be in three years? Will you and your child even remember it? Use these questions to assess if something is worth breaking confidence over. And take even your littlest one's confidences very seriously. They are people too and their trust can be hurt too.

Practice Follow-Through

A child trusts you to deliver on his needs. If you fail to do this, you teach him that he is of little importance to you. You also teach him that he can't rely on you. This will disintegrate a parent-child bond very rapidly. You want to practice follow-through and teach your child to rely on you.

For instance, if you say that you will be at his game on Saturday, you better try your very best to go. If you say that you will talk about something later, then be sure to bring it up later. Make a note if you have to in order to remind yourself. Strive to always fulfill your commitments and promises to your child. Sometimes you will unfortunately fail; that is not the end of the world. You can make up for it later. But keep in mind that a broken promise is a good way to hurt your bond. It is best to never break one if you can help it.

Be There for His Moments

Your child will have some crowning moments in his life. These moments include when he learns to ride a bike without training wheels, when he learns to tie his shoes, when he graduates kindergarten, when he graduates high school and later college, when he goes to prom, etc. For a girl, the first period is often another one of those big moments. You want to be there for these moments and get lots of pictures. This shows that you care a lot. It also lets your child feel important for a day. And you will love having lots of photos to look back on as you notice your child turn into an adult. Childhood is actually very brief.

Try to React with Rationality, Not Anger

Sometimes your kids will hit you with zingers. Your teen informs you that she is having sex, your adolescent informs you that boys at school play a dirty game, your child gets into big trouble at school or with the law, or your child begins to experiment with drugs. These are just some of the countless things that you may be hit with. It is always unpleasant to find out bad things about your child. You may feel that your trust has been broken and that your child is not someone that you really know very well. You may also wonder if you have failed as a parent.

But while anger and disappointment are very common, they will not help if you want a stronger bond with your parents. Your kids won't want to tell you anything if they think, "My mom/dad will kill me!" The best thing that you can do is react with calmness and rationality when you get hit with a real zinger. You can even take some time away, to breathe and process. Just don't lash out in anger.

Instead, try to teach your child to come to you first by reacting calmly. Don't yell or raise your voice. Don't hit. Don't banish your child to his room for a century and shut off his phone and take away his laptop. You can set up a reasonable punishment, but first, you need to talk this over with your child in a calm and reasonable way. Always walk away if your anger starts to take over. You don't want that to be your driving emotion.

When you sit and talk things over with your child before calmly assigning consequences, you teach your child that he can actually come to you and talk to you about things. He will be less likely to keep secrets and lie. When he starts to fall into a bad crowd, experiment with substances like alcohol, or having sex, he can feel more comfortable telling you. Then you can be more involved in his life and prevent him from making really bad choices.

Think back to when you were a kid. Did super harsh punishments really stop you from doing what you wanted? Did you experiment and do some bad things? Most likely, the answers are no and yes respectively. So keep this in mind when you are dealing with the same behavior in your child. Use introspection to help you manage your child's behavior and experimentation.

Find Out what He/She Loves

What does your child ultimately love? Find out what he is into and express an interest. You may not be into the same things as he is, but by expressing an interest and asking him questions about his action figures or music, you convey that you care. Kids will feel more open around parents who show an active interest in their lives.

Plus, you can bond better with your child by taking him out to do something that he really loves when you two spend quality time together. You can also throw in something that you love. So here's an example. Let's assume that you are a woman with a five-year-old daughter who loves ponies. For a mother-daughter outing, you take her to get ice cream, then take her to a petting zoo, pony zoo, or store that sells My Little Pony and I Love Pony. Then, you two go to your favorite nail salon and you get a pedicure in while she gets her nails painted glittery pink. Perfect, right? That's the ultimate in bonding. You pursued her interests but also taught her to enjoy spending time doing what other people enjoy. And you both had a great time.

You will not always understand what your child likes or does. You may have absolutely no interest or even tolerance in some things. It is OK to roll your eyes at Frozen and plug your ears when the choruses play on new pop dirges. But at least show an interest. Tolerate it for a while, for the sake of your child.

Encouragement

Your child bounds in, excited to the max about winning a game with his friends, and you tell him that his silly street games are not important. Your child gets a B in a subject he struggles in and you tell him that A's are better. Your child expresses interest in becoming a veterinarian and you tell him that there is no way he will be able to get into vet school or be able to afford college. Your child talks about someday getting a Lamborghini and you tell him that only the rich drive Lamborghinis. In these subtle ways, you are tearing down your child's dreams, without even meaning to. How can you expect to have a good bond with your kid if you are constantly criticizing him and tearing down his excitement? You may not mean to do this, but it is a bad habit that you may have learned from your own parents or that you have developed unintentionally as a response to stress in your life. You really need to replace your criticism and negativity with positivity and encouragement.

Don't Bad Mouth the Other Parent

Bad mouthing the other parent is a really common habit, in both married and separated homes. You may be irritated with your partner or ex, so you want to say bad things and complain in front of your child. You may also have hurt feelings about your ex and you hate him or her, so you try to poison your child's image of him or her with mean talk. But understand that this tears down your bond with your child while also making him doubt the goodness of his other parent. In addition, you are teaching him that it is OK to be spiteful and vindictive after a split. As good as it may feel to complain to your kid, take the high road and never speak a bad word about the other parent. If you feel the need to vent, go to a counselor or talk to a friend where your child is not in earshot.

Some parents believe in full disclosure and total openness. This is fine, too, if you prefer to keep things open. You can discuss your feelings with your child and be honest about the problems in your marriage or relationship. However, you should keep in mind that is actually not your child's business. You may disclose this information as you want, but you don't need to impart it. If you do choose to be open in this way, then try to speak about your problems objectively and keep bitterness, spite, hate, and vengeance out of your speech.

Dealing with the Other Parent's Unkindness

You may face the opposite problem, where your child's bond with you is fractured by the other parent's talk. This is a particularly common problem in divorce, where the child spends time with the other parent and hears terrible things about you. He may become distant from you as the other parent coaches him to hate you. Nothing can pierce your heart more than experiencing unfair rejection at the hands of your child. First of all, you must keep in mind that your child is not at fault, but is rather the victim. Second, keep in mind that you can repair your child's bad view of you over time.

The best thing to do in this situation is to continue to try your best to be a good parent. Use the tips above to always make your child feel loved and wanted. Try to disprove what the other parent says through your actions.

If your child mentions what the other parent has said, don't react by bashing the other parent or expressing your anger. Rather, thank your child for telling you about this. Then go on to explain that this is simply not true and you hope that your child will decide for himself that you are not the bad guy. Explain that you and the other parent both have your flaws and the other parent is probably just angry. Explain that he or she says mean things about you to feel better. Even if your child is very young, you will be surprised at how smart kids are. He will probably understand and will use this information to make a better decision about your character.

It is also important to try to work on your bond with the other parent. The other parent may not be cooperative and there is only so much that you can do. However, you should sometimes swallow your pride for your child's sake. Do what you can to make the bond at least civil. Ask the other parent to please consider your child and to try to work things out for the child's sake. You can't force the other parent to do anything, but you may be able to influence his or her behavior for the better. If you keep the focus on the child, you can remind the other parent to be an adult and put personal feelings aside for the child.

Sometimes, family counseling can be very beneficial. The entire family must go, including the other parent's new spouse, your new spouse, and any stepchildren that either of you may have. You all need to work together to raise your child. You are still a family, even if you are separated from your child's other parent. If you are still with the child's other parent, it is even more important to work through your differences and try to work your issues out in the best way possible. Don't feel above marriage counseling or going to a pastor or rabbi for marriage advice if you are religious.

Chapter 7: Setting Boundaries with Your Child

You love your child. However, this hardly means that he or she gets to rule your life. Setting boundaries can mean the difference between your sanity and losing your mind while trying to parent. It can also mean the difference between great parenting and poor parenting. Boundaries are important to set up with any person in your life, including your child.

Your Child is not the Most Important Person in the Family

You may have just read that subtitle and thought, "Seriously? What kind of horrible parenting book did I just pick up?" Before you get upset, hear me out. This subtitle is a strong one. Your child is probably your world. He is probably the reason that you wake up in the morning and the reason that you go to work. Your life revolves around him. How can he not be the most important person in the family?

However, this very attitude is what makes many parents burn themselves out. Of course your child is important. Of course he is precious. I am not suggesting that you make him any less so. What I am suggesting is that you adjust your attitude about the importance of other things and people in your life. Your child is important but other people and things are too. Your child should not be *most* important at all times.

Too many parents make their child number one and forget about everything and everyone else. This is just an unfortunate truth about parenting. But if you keep the attitude that your child is only here because of you and the other parent, you are able to assign importance to other people in your life who are of great importance too. You stop neglecting yourself, your partner, your friends, and your family members as you obsess over your child.

Your child is of utmost importance. He needs your love and care. But he should not take center stage in your life and make you forget about everyone else. He does not need to be the center of attention all of the time. In fact, by sometimes turning your attention elsewhere, you teach your child the valuable lesson that he is not the only person in your life who matters. This will help him learn respect and boundaries, and it will help him form a healthy ego.

Spending some time with your child is essential, absolutely. But your child can safely spend some time alone. He can also spend some time with friends, or with other family. This will help him develop a healthy and normal social life, where he is not one hundred percent reliant upon you for all of his entertainment. You can take some time off to focus on yourself and your partner.

As I said in Chapter 5, it is very important to make time for you and your partner. And as I said in Chapter 4, you need to make time for yourself as well. But don't forget the rest of the world, either. It is perfectly all right for you to leave your child with the grandparents or a sitter or your spouse so that you can go out with friends. It is also OK to continue doing the hobbies and crafts that you really love, or to pursue your career. Many parents feel guilty about "neglecting" their children to follow their dreams and passions or spend time with family and friends, but this is ridiculous. You are not here on this Earth only to be a parent. You have an identity outside of parenting. And your child does not need you 24/7/365, as much as he would like for you to think so.

You do not have to wait for your child to reach school age to start living your life outside of parenting. You don't ever have to give up that life. Your child is important, yes, but he doesn't have to be the most important thing in your life, the thing that your life centers around. You can continue to be yourself and lead a life away from your child. Your child will actually grow up healthier if he sees you adopting this healthy attitude about preserving your identity and letting him find his own identity in time away from you.

This is not to say that your child does not need any time with you. Of course he does. You need to be there for him during his important moments. You need to be there to show him that you love him, and to impart wisdom and teach him how to be a good person. You need to be there to listen to him and to help him through his problems. But you do not need to be his slave, at his beck and call. You certainly don't need to be there all the time, smothering him and preventing him from developing his own sense of self.

Make a life outside of parenting. You will notice that your feeling of losing your mind greatly lessens.

No Means No

If you want your child to respect you, then you have to earn that respect. You can't spoil your child and expect him to respect and obey you. Many parents do not believe that children are just here to obey. It is a rising trend for parents to raise their children with empathy and love, rather than by breeding respect and obedience into them.

But there are a few problems with this compassionate style of parenting. Let's say you are in a parking lot, and your child rushes out into oncoming traffic. If you scream "Stop!" then a child who obeys you will come running back to you. You just helped save his life because you have taught him that you know best and that he needs to listen to you. If you scream "Stop!" and he isn't obedient, he may continue running forward and he may get struck by a car. So making sure that your child respects your word as law is actually very important. It is how you can make your child listen to you and learn from you. It is how you can ensure that your child doesn't hurt himself, and that he takes your advice and learns the lessons that you impart to him so that he becomes a good person when he grows up.

In addition, obedience and respect are essential for when a child enters the workforce. Really, it becomes important when your child enters school. He will have a teacher, and later a boss, who fully expects him to do what he is told. If he has not learned from his parents to honor and respect his superiors, then he will not fare very well in the real world. He will find himself in a lot of trouble at school and probably fired from work. So teaching your child respect and obedience is not wrong and it is not cruel. It is essential.

The best way to make your children respect you is to back up what you say with actions. For instance, if you say no, then stand by that no. Don't break down and say yes later just because your child makes the cutest face when he is pouting. It can be tempting, but you need to earn that respect. No always means no. Another example is if you tell your child not to do something, and he does it anyway, then you need to provide some sort of negative consequence to teach him to listen to you in the future. How you choose to punish your child, and also reward him for good behavior, is up to you. But you must develop some sort of system to prove that you mean business. If you don't, you won't earn your child's respect and obedience, and he will be able to walk all over you. You won't ever be able to set boundaries in place.

By earning your child's respect, you become able to set boundaries that your child will adhere to. These boundaries are not just rules. They are lines of interaction that your child simply cannot cross. You have the right to set any boundaries that you see fit. Don't feel selfish for asking for some space and time to yourself, for instance. Don't feel bad about setting up a rule where your child may not interrupt you while you are talking on the phone, unless of course it is a matter of life or death. You can make your bedroom or another area of the house where you don't want your child to go off-limits so that you can have some personal space. You can set rules that say that your child may not bother you or walk in on you while you are using the bathroom. Any boundary that you think is fit is acceptable to put in place.

When you set a boundary, it needs to be hard and fast. Your child will learn that he doesn't have to obey you if you are inconsistent about boundaries or easily give in and give up on boundaries. Your lesson in respect will fail and your boundaries will no longer be taken seriously by your child. Once you make a boundary, it needs to stick. You need to see it through to the end. Eventually, the fight will end and your child will respect your boundaries without having to be told.

Don't feel guilty for setting boundaries. Also don't feel guilty for offering your child consequences for crossing or invading your boundaries. Just be sure to thank your child when he does respect boundaries, to offer him positive affirmation for his good behavior. By setting boundaries, you are taking back your space and your rights as a human being. You are also teaching your child the valuable lesson of respect. Punishing your child for violating boundaries and rewarding him for respecting them will only solidify the lesson for him and help him make sense of your rules.

This is probably one area of parenting where you and your partner are in disagreement. Usually one parent is more lax than the other. Just because your partner doesn't set a certain boundary doesn't mean that you can't. Your child will learn to respect your boundaries, regardless of whether or not your partner enforces them. Don't let your partner drive you crazy; if he or she is not setting the same boundaries that you are, this does not mean that all of your work and effort has gone to waste. Also don't let your partner make you give up on the boundaries that you set. Your child must continue to respect your rules, no matter how different those rules are with his other parent. If your child argues with you and says, "But Mom/Dad lets me do that," you can simple respond, "But I'm not Mom/Dad."

He Doesn't Get to Make the Rules

So many parents feel that they are going crazy because they let their children rule the roost. Their children get to make the rules and set the schedule. The parents are basically slaves to their children's demands, giving their children what they want when they want it. They let their lives revolve around their kids and they let their kids tell them what to do. This just spells disaster. Letting your children rule your life in this way teaches them to disrespect you and gives them an unhealthy sense of superiority that will fail them in the real world. Plus, it exhausts you, because your children don't have a sense of empathy yet and don't know when they have pushed past your limits. You may get frustrated and blow up at your demanding children after a while, which is not fair to them because they have never been told that they are misbehaving.

It is time for you to take control. This is where setting boundaries and sticking by your no's tie together and become fundamental to your successful parenting. Your children do not get to run around the house, making demands of you whenever they feel like it. You have every right to demand to be treated with respect. You must make it clear that you are not a servant, here to grant your child's every wish. Your child will speak to you respectfully and he will not ask you to do things for him when you are busy with something else. He will not be free to bring all of his friends over and expect you to make snacks right when you get off of work. He will not be free to tear the house up and create a huge mess that you have to clean up. He will not be allowed to run around the grocery store, touching things and asking you to buy him extra treats that are not on the list and throwing a tantrum when you say no.

You can set a routine that includes snack times. Make it clear that at the store, you will only buy what's on the list, and you may offer to buy your child a special treat if he keeps up the good behavior and doesn't ask for every little thing he sees. Your child can only have friends over when it is OK with you. He must be respectful of your house and he must pick up any messes that he makes himself.

It is up to you if you want to assign chores. Chores can be a great way to teach responsibility and housekeeping at the same time. You are not the only one in the house who has to do everything. Everyone who lives there should contribute some effort to the maintenance and cleaning. However, some parents don't feel right about doling out chores. It is your prerogative. Making your child clean up messes that he creates is not harmful, though. In fact, it teaches your child to take responsibility for his actions.

You do not have to live by your child's schedule, either. You don't have to stay up way past your bedtime because your child refuses to sleep. Instead, create a schedule that your child must adhere to. Have a regular bedtime as well as regular mealtimes. Also introduce calming activities before bedtime so that your child will go to sleep. After a certain age, you no longer need to be there for your child as he falls asleep. Let him know that lights out is at a certain hour and that he may not get up and wander around the house, come into your room, or otherwise create disruptions after lights out unless he truly doesn't feel well. Being scared of the dark is no reason for you to let your child sleep in your bed and keep you up for hours comforting him. Buy a nightlight and tell him that monsters don't exist and leave it at that.

That is another thing that many parents let their children dictate: sleeping. You have the right to your own bed. You have the right to enjoy sleep, sex, and other activities with your partner in the privacy of your bedroom. You shouldn't have to sacrifice your sex life and your sleep by letting your child sleep in the bed. If you choose to co-sleep with your baby or toddler, that is fine. You are welcome to let your child sleep with you as long as you are comfortable with it. But if it makes you uncomfortable or otherwise interferes with your life, then by all means, stop allowing your child to share your bed with you and your partner. This is a matter that you are allowed to decide on your own. You are not a bad parent if you don't want to co-sleep with your kids, and you're not a bad parent if you like co-sleeping. Each family is different and has different needs. Just do what feels best for you without guilt.

It is also OK to demand that you have some time to watch what you want on TV. Your kid can have his TV hour or a few hours even, but then he needs to go outside and play, or go play with toys in his room. You have the right to watch what you want when you feel like it. Don't let your child dictate when and what you get to watch. Thankfully you can now record TV on most satellite and cable plans, so you can record what you want for later and you can also record your child's favorite shows for later. Nobody has to miss a program. Ultimately, though, you are the adult and you own the TV so you can determine when your child gets to watch it and when you do. Your child does not have a say in this matter.

The same goes for the phone and Internet. You are the boss here. You can limit what sites your child visits and you can limit the amount of time he can talk to his friends. When you need the phone or Internet, you are more than welcome to take it over. Don't let your child rule the roost by giving into his phone and Internet demands. Whether or not you let your child have his own devices is up to you, but you can limit his time and exposure on those devices all you want.

It is best to block certain sites and disable picture messaging for younger children to prevent what they are exposed to.

When it comes to friends, you can allow friends over or not. You can also determine who your child gets to play with and you can limit his contact with certain bad children that you don't want around. Again, this is your house, and you can place rules on who comes in and out of it. Your child doesn't get to decide that. In fact, as a parent, it is your duty to protect your child from certain bad influences, so you are expected to keep him from certain bad friends.

These boundaries don't change with age, unless you want them to. You still rule the roost, even if your child is now an adult living with you. You can demand that your child has the lights out by a certain hour, doesn't make messes, and doesn't have certain people over at certain times, if at all. Your house is still your house, even if your child is an adult. Adult children may pay some of the bills, but they still don't get to boss you around. They could be in their own place or living on the streets, but you let them live with you, so they need to respect your rules and make your home comfortable for you. They don't get to violate the routine that you like.

You can basically lay down the law with your children . What you say goes. Your child does not get to make the decisions or demand anything from you. He does not have an explicit rights to privileges like TV or Internet or even having friends over. Instead, those are treats that he gets for good behavior. By taking control, you can greatly limit how much your child drives you crazy with demands, messes, and hogging TV or other devices.

When Boundaries Go Too Far

You may worry that you are too strict or that certain boundaries are not OK. Usually, any boundary that you see fit is reasonable. But here are some guidelines to help you avoid going overboard:

This is your house. But your child lives here too. He needs at least some space to play and spread out his toys. It is unfair to not let him have space and freedom to be a kid at least somewhere in the home.

You have the right to your own time, but you cannot expect to never spend time with your child. This is neglect and it will hurt your child's development. Spend at least an hour playing with your child and an hour reading a book together. Also try to have a sit-down family dinner at least once a week, where you all share what you have experienced throughout the day and what is new in your lives. Taking your child along on your errands can be a pain, but it can also help expose your child to the outside world, which can help further his development. You can take an hour to yourself for a yoga class, or ask for some time to unwind in your bedroom with a book or your phone after work, but be sure to spend time with your kids too. Scheduling time can help you make sure that you have time for your kids, without letting your kids dictate when you spend time with them.

It is perfectly acceptable to demand that your child remains quiet at times, such as when you are on the phone. But if you are on the phone for most of the day, you owe it to your child to spend some time with just him. Don't look at your phone or take calls during your time with your child. Treat this time is like a date or meeting; it is very important for you to pay attention and give it your all.

It is also acceptable to expect your child to be quiet during certain times, but that doesn't mean that you can just ignore him. Children need constant supervision, especially if they are under ten. Keep an eye and an ear on him at all times. Should your child get hurt or truly need help, he comes before the phone conversation or your nap.

You can stand by your boundaries. Just make sure that your child's safety comes first. Also make sure to make yourself available to your child for talking and bonding. Your child won't be this little ever again, so cherish as much time with him as you can. Your life doesn't have to revolve around him, but at least make him the biggest part of your life.

What Other People Say

You will never be the perfect parent. And plenty of people out there are more than happy to remind you of that fact. You will encounter tons of people who will criticize your parenting. It is important to set a boundary with them as well. Otherwise, these people will drive you even crazier than your beloved child does!

It is perfectly OK to defend yourself and tell other people to mind their own business. No one is an expert, so what other people say is not necessarily correct. Just because someone has the nerve to criticize your parenting does not mean that he or she is right in his or her criticism. Learn to take what everyone says with a grain of salt. You can smile and pretend to take their advice, or you can put your foot down. Either way, you should not let other people bully you and drive you nuts with their countless different opinions about how you should raise your child.

Don't let people boss you around. Say what you need to in order to get them off of your back. You can say things like, "Let's not talk about this." You can even say things like, "Please don't tell me how to raise my child. Thanks!" You don't have to get mad, as anger rarely helps in any situation. But you should be intolerant of this meddling.

The parenting style that resonates with you the most is the style that you should adopt. Only do what feels right to you. Parenting is also a matter of trial and error. You might have a plan in place while you are pregnant or in the adoption process, and that plan goes to smithereens once you actually have a real child in your life. You will find out that certain discipline tactics or rewards do not work while others do. Over time, as you get to know your child and as you and your child both grow as people, you will figure out what works best. Don't let others fill your head with conflicting nonsense and convoluted tips that do not apply to your situation or do not seem agreeable to you.

More than anything, you need to take care of yourself. If you are not taken care of, who will take care of your child? This is why being a little bit selfish at times and putting yourself first is not wrong. It is actually beneficial to your precious little one in the long run. Other people may criticize you for going out or making time for yourself and having date nights with your partner, but they are just being meddlesome. Don't ever feel bad for taking care of yourself and your romantic relationship. A child does not mean that your entire life goes on hold and everything becomes about the child.

Chapter 8: Keep a Positive Mindset

One piece of advice that many veteran parents will tell you is: Keep a sense of humor. Why is this so important? Because laughing at things, rather than being serious all of the time, will help you preserve your sanity. Try to make light of things and make parenting fun.

The mindset that you have about parenting will help you tremendously. You need to have a positive mindset to enjoy parenting and make it through the bad times well. Clear your head, learn to focus on the positive, and keep a sense of humor about things.

When your baby has a blowout, it's embarrassing and terrible to clean up. But if you laugh about it, that will make it better. If your child plays the same Sesame Street Elmo toy songs over and over, you may want to rip that toy to shreds. Instead, laugh about it and recognize how cute kids are. When your child throws a fit, record it and show it to friends with kids later, or use it as a form of birth control to convince your kids not to have unprotected sex and get pregnant young.

When you find that the going gets tough, use your love for your child as motivation to press on. You are here to raise a kid. You want to enjoy and treasure the experience. You want to treat your child well and help him flourish into a wonderful adult. Your desire to see your child succeed and your desire to be a good parent are both great motivators that can help carry you through anything.

Conclusion

Having a child is the best thing that can happen to you. But it can also spike your stress levels and make you feel crazy! Any parent will understand what I mean by this. With the advice in this book, you can help simmer down the crazy factor.

Being a parent is not easy. But if you keep a positive mindset and make yourself and your partner priorities, you will do just fine. Releasing anger in a healthy way is also essential so that you don't make a habit of taking your feelings out on your child. Unfortunately, it is often required of parents to set their personal feelings aside for the best interests of their children. This can be hard, but if you remember how much you love your child, you will be more willing to do anything for him or her.

Children are a blessing. But they don't need to rule your life. You can have a life outside of your parenting. In fact, it is beneficial to do so. Your children are important but so is your health, your love life, your job, and other parts of your life. Life doesn't stop once you have a baby if you don't let it. Continue to take care of yourself and your romantic relationship as if they are of equal importance to your child.

Whether you gave birth or adopted your child, you are now a parent. That is scary but it is also wonderful. Try to focus on the positive. Use your love for your child as motivation to get through the hard times. Use your child as a reason to get up in the mornings, even when it is hard. He depends on you and needs you. He also loves you very much.

Thank you for reading.

Other books available by K.W. Williams on Kindle, paperback and audio

Lifting The Clouds: How To Support A Loved One With Depression

Meditation 101: Beat the Stress with the Power of Your Mind

The Science of Self Massage: Independently Relieve Stress Using
Techniques That Target Trigger Points

Personality Decoder: Identifying and Maneuvering Around Different
Personality Styles